# PHILIP QUAITE

# Let Winter pass thru you

To Joan
From Pip

**Belfast**

**LAPWING**

First Published by Lapwing Publications
c/o 1, Ballysillan Drive
Belfast BT14 8HQ

Copyright © Philip Quaite 2001

British Library Cataloguing in Publication Data.
A catalogue record for this book
is available from the British Library.

Set in Aldine 721 BT
by
Winepress Services

ISBN 1 898472 52 1

# CONTENTS

# Let Winter pass thru you

To the painting, once again,
Your eye, your brushstrokes;
A wash of thick dense ink
        Shadows and shades
Upon hills with heavy rains

But then, Angel,
You've lost your wings
And what with night ahead
So sensitive
Easy to pull apart like a flower

Do you remember
When all the partying and music
Blasted sheer from your room
And all thru the house
People joined hands
And prayed for the evil spirits
To pass out of you

Then, hold your head in your hands,
Let Winter pass thru you

# Contemplating Exorcism

Graveyard cough in the chill
Spit in the puddle where moonlight
Plays with naked winter'd trees

So let it be, this ritual beneath holy Oak Eve
Make all voices leave me forever.
Oh Let ye demons depart

She rises from Roses in the garden,
Fills the coalbucket and plays with the dog
As Mingus and his big band swings in -

0h What Blues until my head is so sad;
Banging about; all points to nothing
And that evil spirit not gone yet

## Just Blown in, Precious

Let the breezes blow thru all paper walls
Let the Birds all out of their cages.
0! Yes! We loved the big grass we loved in
And the old Lighthouse beams were
Like strobes and smokebombs upon our Rave,
You a girl with a sweet druggy smile
With loud laughter all mixed up in chaos
And will out! Will Out! From star to star!
Me, too demented to buy you a ring —
0h Higher than birds!

Her arm draws across the curtains
She asks after you
Must be near enough a Century loose


## Miracle

There she danced in the lights and smoke
Until the whole house turned around and around;
She put her web all about me

All night upon tops of rain clouds
As high and as safe as Heaven;
Like snakes, we cast old skins for new

And the tiny Cross bled from the Heart
Across the mantelpiece and down the wall;
Surely 'tis time for a Miracle

# Midday Cut

In a bright room, asleep,
Shadows sharp and Midday cut
In a chair your back to the window
Where I can see the sea and ships passing by
It's ghostlike, surreal and totally déjà vu
Strange moments in lifeknot made loose

And random thoughts
Like the bells of Notre-Dame thru me
— We didn't know what day it was
And had only one Franc stepping into the city;
Hare Krishna monks fed us
And I begged for Cigarette money
The ladies of the streets were honeys
And asked us in.

Why am I thinking about old times really in Paris?
My father! Do you want my life story, really?

Say, it's gentle and soft in here,
Look at the white horses out to sea.
No voices raised;
Old people trying to get out of chairs for Lunch

# The Passing

Breath becoming slow and slight,
You turned your head slowly;
Saying Good bye, sleeping away,
7:10 a.m. outside, a storm howled
Blowing the Cherry tree blossom like snowflakes
All in cold morning clutch
With a grey dawn breaking, Spring awakening
And I wondered where you were —
Somewhere on the earth yet somewhere in Heaven?

Blackbirds sing shrill thru drawn blinds
The needle in the Barometer points to change,
Strange change indeed Just like that!
Blowing a blossom off my hand

## Sonnet

0! pray for the birds to sing again around the place
Has too much woe shut them up? and who did wrong?
And you feel harm, confusion and guilt
But it was my guts to yours, I swear it,
How I dig the memory of some old scene between us,
Tender and gentle, cushioning me from cruel existence.
Trying to make sense I pick up Shakespeare's Sonnets —
Of Times ravages; Youth to old age.
He says, get thee with child a comely maid
Before its too late and you sink with hate of yourself
and very life.

Again I say, Old Age is peeping around the corners,
I saw him in a few places, last year gone by;
Well? What of it! if the Reaper sharpens his scythe.

## Someone had been talking about the crematorium

Blue Tits hanging from the bird-table
Thru rain upon January gardens
Against radiator by Bungalow window
Someone had been talking about the crematorium
And remembering clear and clean,
The coffin disappearing into the incinerator.
Cold May, yet with a washout sun blazing.
It sat in your room, the little Urn of your ashes,
I sat there too with your welcome ghost.
This is personal and in trust; still miss you badly
And things that came to me - a silver tankard,
Photographs, Penknife, Box with Compasses
And particular favourite ghost haunting your bedroom
Thru dull of day, don't go in there at night.
Lo! it all ends in a wooden box
Up the road in a black shiny Hearse

## That side of Madness

His Madness set in with the making of the Loom
& the perfect Guitar but with faults you had to remedy.
I watched you collapse then & saw so many things
In your insane stare, yes, stay well away
With a curse into the fire with spit,
Paranoia, Fear; an Ogre or a mad Bear's look,
No more medicine, why you've even forgotten prayers
To the Earth Mother


## For Theolonius Monk

I'd been filling up the bins with the empties
The Crows have gone home to roost
I'm whistlin "Nutty" —
Been listenin to Theolonius play all day,
Watchin out the window the comin's and goins of the Crows,
Tapping my feet to the riffs up and down the magic keys.
If the band hadn't come in just then
You'd still be pounding the Ivories forever
In the Baroness's music room,
Better acoustics anyhow than Carnegie or Philharmonic,
All comfort here, all pain too
And the music sending me

                                    out the window
                                    over the hills;
                                    soul of a night Crow

# Salt in it

You missed all   the beautiful lightning
                out over the sea
And the gentle rain of the day
While a broken string on your Violin
             maddened me.
How I love when the wind out of the storm
Whips at you tangling your hair all up,
              madness not far away
And all those system tranqs cannot
           bring you down enough.
Your beauteous Imagination weeps,
Frustrated, sick and sad
Ace of Spades always falling your way


# China the Tom

By the fire like King Lion
The Cat so impressive and cool
Diggin all the Jazz.
Slate grey and such bright shiny eyes,
I can reassure myself happy here
With this reincarnation of an ancient Pharaoh,
Spooky grey with three legs;
Dog tore off a leg and most off his tail
Can't scratch himself there now when he wants to
Always here by the fire
0! China! 0! Incredible wall of China
Where I will walk with you tonight,
Sleek and rapid Catman

## Dream resulted in game of Russian Roulette

Sprinkle the cadence of a cold dawn
All over y'r forehead, cold drips from the tap;
After all hunting put on y'r Wolf-mask
And Dance to the drums over all relics.

Polish it! Polish it! Go it man!
Do the tango from Mallaig to Marrakesh
0! all ye unknown Buenos Aires brothel dancers,
Out unto new Promontories! Into unknown seas!

Upon awakening
I pick up and finger up tobacco,
Hold gun to temple in morning penance.

# The Glue-Sniffer's Joke

Down sittin on the subway steps;
Denim, bright red pallor,
Can of adhesive, dirty plastic bag,
— "Is there anyone down there?"
He asked in a shaky voice,
Glued-up eyes staring madly into the subway.
No, I replied, only the horrors of southern slave-mines
And the ghosts of perverted Graffiti artists

— "Need help! need help!"
I'm a terrorist! I'm a terrorist!
" Ha! Ha! Ha! Been readin a comic!"
Freaked at his intense frolic and otherworldly calm
Banging the Corporation Street evening down in a fist,
I hurried away, a little afraid.

# Xmas Eve

i say third tyme        bomb riddance robot come down road
                         bomb riddance robot unlucky
                         go up in smoke

maybe no tyme to call in robot
bomb casually placed beneath a seat
timed to detonate — 10:30 Xmas Eve
shall i saunter across for a quiet pint this Xmas Eve
for a quiet pint
for a quiet thought
only Proboscis Monkey know
and he no concerned —

                         he stay happy in the jungle

                         he no wanna know

# Having a Fix in the derelict Maternity Unit

So this,
            The place that the pregnant women all came to
Utter grey upon grey, unwashed walls and dusty windows,
shutting in that miracle of Birth, shutting everything
                                            else out,
— An entire History of the screams of Labour.
These very large washhand basins
Sprouting out of the walls like Surreal vegetables;
Obscene, weird, all in correct delft, white and dusty,
With brown stains and Spider's webs.
Just to bathe pregnant women!
New-born babes in the midst, connecting up here
Far the first time in this nothing place.
Neither crying babes nor Angels' faces brought me here,
This is where we sit in a queue, all us "Nuts"
Holding our little boxes of Ampoules,
System drugs in sweaty fiddling hands;
"Breath in —— That's it —— Here's a bandage —
—— Yr bleeding a bit."
Ranting and raving about all the grey Erotica!
Split fast for the morning air.

## "Us big girls know best how to keep you cosy"

I want to thread your fine white hair
Thru my Venetian blinds,
I'll work a strange loom here in my room
Your beauty trapped at my whims and devices,
O never mind the dog barking
Or voices of the sick and old
Raised aloud in anger about the rents and taxes

Bright wings of Angels beating about
And village voices high and low
In a melody like the sound of falling snow,
Then you say with a sexy laugh —
"Us big girls know best how to keep you cosy".
All this and what else on a winter morning.

Why now, I wonder, do you leave wounds
Upon me that can't be closed up?
Nothing, ever happened to us before.

## Madame Rose ponders back

O constant mistress let a moon bleed boldly
On gates to all sweet meadows
Where you'll see all manner of strangeness
You'll hardly be able for it;
The deep manic truth.
You may wear a dagger
But all the life's gone out of your swagger
With your Barbarella boots and your black tights
Your Liquorice sticks and Lucozade for breakfast
While you ponder over the great matter of your lovers
And what you can't remember from the night before
Which is dangerous for someone thinkin on murder,
Another Winter gone down on sinister arrangements
With men totin guns while at the same time
They come across with what you want
Dead on the frozen hourbell
Of the perfect finished number.

# Lines for K

They're were Diamonds around your neck
As bright as big raindrops
On first Catkins of Willows.
And i saw you there in Heartbreak House
Doin' the heavy Cinderella bit,
Down on your knees cleanin' out the grate
In the grey stoned morning.
"Wrecked this morning
And getting stoned again."
Stand on the sands
And miss out thru time,
Out unto the hills
Shoulder the stormbent Hawthorn,.
Seeing reflections in puddles
That would dazzle ye in your Summer light
And the old Doss-house gaped on down the street
And was heartbroken at you leavin'.

## Incident, New Year's Day

It was quiet except for the talk and crack
— Then it started —
"I'm gonna head-butt that pendulum hard."
As he fought with the Grandfather clock around the room
Banging and bloodying his fists until the clock
Fell on the floor; such a racket,
"Happy New Year! he yelled, "Happy New Year!"
Then he fell himself, stone drunk on the floor
"Aye! I think he's a screw missin'." Someone said,
As if the clock hadn't.

## Hope

In all the greyness and red brick of the deathhouses
The shining faces of the Madonnas
Who set the Wicked out by the door forever

Its still, still beneath the stars
With Angels in at all windows
Why chase after a mountain when a mountain comes

They're throwing cinders on the dirt
Nymphs arising from evening pools with ease and calm
Is the land gay and green again this Eve, or do I dream?

# In the Paranoid Hour & Orgasm

By the saddest of rivers I listened
'To the chanting of the Priests, beneath
                         the gentle Hazel;
0! Nadima, you were the fairest in all the country
                         south to Tintagel & tonight
Your heart becomes one with the moon & sun
                         as the fine blade slices.
Well may the Bards measure beats on the Harp,
                         songs from the heart,
'Tis of no avail; thy bosom i yearn for
Yet Weird's way is, thy blood for the Sun.

Mouth stained with Mead & Dingleberry
I walked back to the village
From the place of your last ecstatic scream;
Along the way i picked Woodbine;
Sweetness in Sorrow, Joy all fallen.
They wrapped your body by rapids
Alive & eddy fulsome as the running stream
As when in. our Spring we loved
Along the Rose-bridges by the cliffs,
Kinsmen grave made kindest wordplay
They do not know that i return when Moon be full
To stare upon her face, her hair with the ripples
                         mixing wildly — golden fresh
The waters take care of their Priestess
Forever & forever without end.

"Get back! get back! ten hundred years"
                              the Vision cries:
Spring's bosques have blossomed rotten.
                                   'Tis a season of such hate
& to think that Christ walked here
                         just a moment ago.
Now he's returned to the depths of the jungle.


Late smeared with young girl's blood
A black Moth of hairy gigantic size
Makes its way into my tiny room
                              with hideous intent
Fast as a Gun towards my eyes —
            — Another pig of a riot cop
                His kiss of Love is a tear-gas bomb

Chaos Reincarnate
After Arthur Rimbaud


So it begins.
By Mereside the horns adorned mouths it's
                    clear stark note
Travellers in the borderlands beware!

I bequeath you Love, a white kitten for Xmas,
                    — A great white Puma
                    That will haunt the northern wastes
Then! Then! Scop of the four o'clock Poems,
                    Weird maker in Limbo,
The only darkness, after having perfected
                    the substance,
Will be my Puma's eyes —
                    dark deep eyes
                    afloat in the snow

Look! the kittens drowned
Become the sweet Blackbird's singing
In the forlorn. gardens by the madhouse wall,
Torture of Life!
And the sad Butterfly will never fly again,
First frosts of Winter eating into it's tortoise
                    wings

Damn it! The Butterfly is alive!
It is the fire you see burning in. the Ice
0! Ecstasies of flame forever!

## El Tosemoros

By rocks of pitched dream and maddest heart;
Snow rage, sea green,
Faint dim disc of Sun above,
Where the guitar and lament of El Tosemoros
Joins with birdcry and tide din.

El Tosemoros! my silver haired one! my gypsy Guru!
Musician of Blue beach, feet lapped by the sea.
I slide under his strings to a beautiful sleep,
All nature fading except his hands at their stringing.

— An eternal love song
  O! Lament until frozen

# The White Flowers

As i was walking in the gloomy prison gardens
I came across a bank of white flowers
And i could see you faraway in another city,
In another country across the sea,
In the little marketplace by your stall,
Amidst your furs and jewels, Saturn twirling
In your eyes, your earrings all-a-jangle
With mad moonlight music
And that night we walked in magic forest glades,
Came to a lake with waters red;
A wondrous barge of golden Elm drifted by,
An eagle sat there on a crystal ball
Feathers white as snow; the bird was softly saying —
          "I am Solomon's bird"
          "In whose woods you walk"
          "I am bird of white feather"
          "I am the Vision of Love."

# Tigonaud

First card —
A soft white Dove with beads of blue Amber in its beak,
Then the card of the Rose, deep deep rouge,
A maid in her castle tower weeping for her lover
Then the mighty Jester, Death and bones.

I sat with you by an ivory table in a magic garden
You dealt two cards, the nine of hearts
                              the nine of hearts again
Our Love sang raging in our veins —
A silver Unicorn, with golden tusk and deep red eyne
Stood beneath a Silver Birch;
I took my lady in my arms
And away we did ride up into the stars,
They're was never a happier threesome;
That night we lay at Love's games
Castle of Ice, on a frozen rainbow
Somewhere in Tigonaud's elfin wilderness
A blood moon shone thru the fairy casement
Like the light from that holy star in the morning skies
That lies on mighty Pharaoh's eyes.

## Street Scene

The Salvation Army band shattered the silence
Of the sunny Sunday afternoon street;
— Busy black coated insects at redface work
With flashing brass, little children
Crashing tambourines tripped and skipped
Along behind, the very image of happiness.
It shattered the street. It shattered our sadness,
We were in love and the question would
Our love come thru? Would it stand?
We were like a tablecloth soaked with Wine
And the street scene like some disgruntled waitress
Noisily rung the Wine out of the tablecloth,
— Splashes of Carnation red upon dirty white tiles.


## But what things to say to Cinderella

Shall I to the tick of your metronome
Set above the ivories of the last Whale
By which the tides of Sin.

Damn it! Set the whole bloody Zoo free!
And all ye fish of the seas poisoned!
No crops and yet we have sacrificed many!

But what things to say to Cinderella,
Nearly midnight, sound of you
Up cobbled streets i cannot follow.

# Sunset

Shadows long down the street
Cries of Starlings
Your laughter
You talked of your schooldays
Becoming monotonous in your Innocence
As if those were better days.
It seemed from your eyes
You were back there in the classroom
Pigtailed, stiff-skirted and boyish
With the old Lesbian teacher feeling around you.
Then trainwindow homewards,
Sunset ocean of colour west over hills
Stiletto memorial to war
In vain and violent silhouette;
We kissed and the whole ruddy sunset
Across the Cavehill in lips joined.
In ten years, twenty, even thirty,
Will my eyes gleam like yours do now
As the memory of this sunset
Flashes on and off
As if those were better days

# Incident, Evening, a hospital ward

Garish lights and Venetian blinds
The usual bad food for tea
A bit of crack among the men
When the shrieks of the bereaved women
Filled the place
Bringing to a hush the ward
As fast as the Death that had just happened.
The old man's family were many and all broken;
Their sobbings ebbed away thru the building
Into the night.
Emotion written thick in the atmosphere
With norm gradient re-establishing itself;
The return of conversation
The Television turned up again
Bottles of Guinness for supper
And the evening visitors,
One pretty young woman was brightly dressed
And slightly Pregnant, bearing
A bunch of Roses.

# Hey! hot Spiritual Mama!

Hey! hot Spiritual Mama!
I need of you tonight,
The horrors again and transgressions,
We will not meet after the Cockfight
And spend all the money on Rum
Though you're very precious
And you've shown me the nine ways
Of how to be a Lizard in my next lifetime.
I dig yr eyes, yr nose and yr taste
For jewellery about yr nakedness,
— What, not even exhausted yet?
Randy Lioness scream at the night
Rip the hip cat on till
He succumbs with one last growl
And all the bush knows
Why even the Witchdoctors know
That tonight big power of hot Spiritual Mama
        has gone down,
Taking with it a love-lorn star from Heaven,
— Star thought he O.K. there

# Rainbowdrops

Rainbowdrops dripping off boughs
To the street where I dance witless
In the Winter eve.

A young girl kicks an empty beer-can to me
I kick it back to her, long hair, fun
And the laugh of an Angel.

It sends the heavy boot away and the head,
— I'm walking Pont-Neuf again into the Latin Quarter
Looking for Love where heart was torn.
Find it, somehow patch it up again
Beat it up again and get drunk on it again
In the empty cafe, only a grotesque whore.

Sickness and hunger in yr bones
I can see its hard for you
To struggle upstream, old Bear.

Anyhow, where are you really going?

# Winter of the heavy boot gone down

Weird ramblings there young Tobias,
And that's a good and dense-full Hookah;
0! lady of Canton, please smile upon me again
When my ship's in that port
As the April showers knock me off my feet
And they're towers and chimneys in plenty for concreting
Winter of the heavy boot gone down.

All up and down the coast
I've been phoning up the antique hotels to find you;
I'll inspire Hawks to find jewels in desert sands
And bring them in deliverance of beak to your tents.
I await a breeze to crackle the canvas of my sails,
My craft is a light one and has speed
And carries all manner of treasure for your eyes
Yeah! even stars forgotten and fallen from Heaven
Winter of the heavy boot gone down.

## Man of Mission

O blow the wind the boat to the cruel shore
Man of Mission,
Sunlight of Summer yet his withered crops
And hoarfrost upon his beard,
Love gone from him forever without doubt
Only the dark millpond and comfortless tower,
All remaining of his once fair land..
Possessed of all virtues truly,
He raged and turned all night
On the mean cruel boards
So that the song of birds at dawn
Became his only happiness
Until no birds sang
And all about was a barren realm,
Blast of the cannon, breath of the Dragon,
Welcome the sup of Poison.

O blow the wind the boat to the cruel shore
Man of Mission

Ω